Exploring Language

RICHARD BAIN

Exploring Language
& POWER

CAMBRIDGE
UNIVERSITY PRESS

Published by the Press Syndicate of the University of Cambridge
The Pitt Building, Trumpington Street, Cambridge CB2 1RP
40 West 20th Street, New York, NY 10011–4211, USA
10 Stamford Road, Oakleigh, Melbourne 3166, Australia

© Cambridge University Press 1993

Photography by Graham Portlock

Illustrations by Maggie Ling (page 10) and Mrinal Mitra (pages 17 and 18)

First published 1993

Printed in Great Britain at the University Press, Cambridge

A catalogue record for this book is available from the British Library.

ISBN 0 521 44626 0 paperback

GO

Acknowledgements

Thanks are due to the following for permission to reproduce from copyright material:

page 4, number 2, reproduced from *Lost for Words* by permission of J W P Creber;
page 6, number 1, reproduced by permission of the Bank of England; page 6, number
2, reproduced by permission of British Rail; page 8, cartoon reproduced by
permission of *Punch*; page 8, 'Four Letters and the Law' from *Dictionary of Slang
and Unconventional English*, reproduced by permission of Cambridge University
Press; page 8, 'Tax tuft cost £60', © *The Guardian*; page 8, 'Youth finally said 'yes'...',
reproduced by permission of the *North Shields News Guardian*; page 9, 'Basque'
from *The Cambridge Encyclopedia of Language* by David Crystal, reproduced by
permission of Cambridge University Press; page 9, number 3, © Cephas Picture
Library; page 10, cartoon reproduced by permission of the *Daily Star*; page 10,
extracts from *Women, Men and Language* by Jennifer Coates, 1986, reproduced by
permission of Longman Group UK; page 11, reproduced by permission of Future
Publishing; page 12, newspaper advertisement reproduced by permission of Fiat Auto
(UK) Limited; page 13, reproduced by permission of the National Union of
Journalists; page 19, reproduced by permission of British Telecom/G-R
Communications Ltd.

Every effort has been made to reach copyright holders. The publishers would be glad
to hear from anyone whose rights they have unknowingly infringed.

Contents

The purpose of this book is to encourage you to collect and explore examples of your own. Please don't just rely on the samples of language in this book.

 # Language at school

1 TEACHER/PUPIL CONVERSATIONS

TEACHER	1939. How many years ago? Where are the mathematicians among you?
PUPIL	43.
TEACHER	43. Well done. It was 43 years ago.

TEACHER	Does anybody know what a 'gallower' is?
PUPIL 1	A jumper, Miss.
TEACHER	No, I said 'gansy' for that.
	(Pause.)
TEACHER	A 'gallower'. I'll write it on the board.
	(Pause.)
TEACHER	Yes?
PUPIL 2	A pony.
TEACHER	Yes, well done, it's a pony.

2 LOST FOR WORDS

BOY	When I was . . .
TEACHER	Say SIR when you speak to a member of staff.
BOY	Sir, . . . I was at . . .
TEACHER	And take your hands out of your pockets. I don't speak to the Headmaster with my hands in my pockets . . .
BOY	Sorry –
TEACHER	. . . or leaning on a radiator.
BOY	Sorry – Sorry, SIR . . . when I was at Blacton . . .
TEACHER	Well, boy, get on with it – when you were at Blacton . . .?
BOY	Yes, Sir, when I was at Blacton Primary School . . . we used to go bird-watching on the cliffs and . . .
TEACHER	Jones, I suppose you realise what this lesson is . . .?

From *Lost for Words* by J. Patrick Creber

3 HANDBOOK FOR NEW PUPILS

YOU SHOULD:

- have with you your pen, pencil and ruler as MINIMUM items of equipment, plus aprons for practical lessons

- remove outdoor clothing before starting school, and hang up coats in the cloakroom provided; coats are NOT to be worn around the school

- arrive promptly for lessons

- wait in a quiet, orderly manner outside the classroom

- enter the room quietly and take your place in a similar manner

- conform to standards of classroom behaviour, which include politeness of speech to ALL, the raising of a hand before asking or answering questions, and non-interference with fellow pupils

- treat textbooks, exercise books, files, etc. with respect and NOT deface them with graffiti

- await dismissal by the teacher and not take the bell as a signal to pack up or leave

- complete work set, INCLUDING homework, promptly

- always keep to the left in the corridors.

From *Handbook for New Pupils*, comprehensive school

Commands and requests

FOR THE HEALTH
AND COMFORT
OF OTHERS
**PLEASE DO NOT
SMOKE**

Please do not
SMOKE

We respectfully ask you
DO NOT SMOKE
in the school building

Thank you

D A N G E R

Propane

**NO SMOKING
NO NAKED LIGHTS**

!
You are
entering a
NO SMOKING
area

No smoking
Penalty £50 Maximum

**THANK YOU FOR
NOT SMOKING**

Language that lets you do things

1 BANKNOTE

2 RAIL TICKETS

BRITISH RAILWAYS BOARD
This ticket is issued subject to the conditions shown in the Board's
current Passenger Conditions of Carriage and also in
other of the Board's publications and notices app
to its use. It is not transferable.
Unless otherwise indicated valid by any reasonable route.

SPECIMEN

Where the symbol '+' appears after the printed destinati
ticket is available for cross-London transfer by LRT Unde
without additional charge, via any recognised route app
to the through BR journey being made.

BR No. 4599   N/3/91/98

Class	Ticket type		Adult	Child	
STD	SUPERSAVER RTN		ONE	NIL	RTN
	Date		Number		
FOR	15 FBY 99A		77706 4603 7729E06		
From			Valid		Price
LONDON BRIT RAIL SEE RESTRICTNS					£39 20X
To			Route		
NEWCASTLE *					1702

SPECIMEN

British Rail

'Bad' language?

1 *PUNCH* CARTOON

Punch cartoon of 2 April 1913 Old Lady: I shouldn't cry if I were you, little man.
Little Boy: Must do sumping; I bean't old enough to swear.

2 FOUR LETTERS AND THE LAW

In 1936, Eric Partridge (1894–1979) included 'fuck' in his *Dictionary of Slang and Unconventional English*. Despite his use of an asterisk for the vowel, the result was a storm of complaints to schools, libraries, and the police. Even today, the book is not always available on the open shelves of public libraries.

The Cambridge Encyclopaedia of Language
David Crystal, Cambridge University Press 1987

3

News in brief

Tax tuft cost £60

A shaven-headed man who had tufts of hair with the words "fuck the poll tax" cut in was fined £60 by magistrates yesterday.

Unemployed Wayne Steventon, aged 21, said after the case: "It's a free country and I think I should be able to say what I like with my haircut. I had a haircut which read 'fuck the police' last week, but I had to shave it off before I came to court."

Magistrates at West Bromwich heard that Mr Steventon was spotted by two police officers in Wednesbury, West Mid-

lands. The words were clearly visible from 20 yards.

Damian Hayes, prosecuting, said: "The officers told Steventon to cover the haircut up because it was offensive, but he refused and was arrested."

Mr Steventon, of Tipton, West Midlands, admitted an offence under the Public Order Act.

He said later: "I'm not going to pay my fine, or my poll tax and I'm planning another offensive haircut. I don't care if they send me to prison for it."

The Guardian

Other languages

1

Youth finally said 'yes' . . .

After initially saying "aye" and refusing to say "yes" to a query from the bench, a 16-year-old youth made a remark as he was leaving the juvenile court at Whitley Bay.

He was removed from the court and taken below to the police station.

The youth had pleaded not guilty to two offences and a trial date had been arranged.

When asked if he understood this, he replied: "aye".

He continued to say "aye" when told he should reply either "yes" or "no".

He eventually said "yes", but left the court muttering.

Before he reached the door, he turned to the magistrates and said, loudly: "I hope you are not on the f . . . ing bench."

He was brought back into the court and marched down the stairs to the police station.

When other cases had been dealt with, he was brought back into court, accompanied by a court usher and a police officer.

Miss Judy Buksmann, representing the youth, said she regretted that one of her clients should have insulted the bench.

She was not familiar with this particular client. If she had been, she would have been alerted.

It was perhaps a reflection of society today, she said, that young people thought one standard of behaviour was applicable for all situations.

She had explained to the youth that a different standard was expected, and could be demanded, in court.

The youth apologised unreservedly, she said.

Asked if he agreed with this, the youth replied: "Yes".

Before being allowed to leave, he was told by the chairman, Mr Geoffrey Orde: "This is a court of law. We are doing a job and expect people who come to court to respect that."

The North Shields News Guardian

2 MIND HOW YOU SAY IT

3

Then Gilead cut Ephraim off from the fords of the Jordan, and whenever an Ephraimite fugitive said 'Let me cross', the men of Gilead asked him, 'Are you an Ephraimite?'. If he answered 'No', they said, 'Then say "Shibboleth."' He would say 'Sibboleth', since he could not pronounce the word correctly. Thereupon they seized and slaughtered him by the fords of the Jordan.

Judges 12, verses 4–6

Basque

The way language can become a symbol of national identity is very clearly seen in the history of Basque (Euskera), and the attitude towards it of the Spanish government under Franco, from 1937 until the mid-1950s. The teaching of the language in schools was forbidden, as was its use in the media, church ceremonies, and all public places. Books in the language were publicly burnt. Basque names were no longer allowed in baptism, and all names in the language on official documents were translated into Spanish. Inscriptions on public buildings and tombstones were removed.

By the early 1960s, official policy had changed. Basque came to be permitted in church services, and then in church schools and broadcasts. In 1968, a government decree authorized the teaching of regional languages at the primary level in Spain. By 1979, the Ministry of Education had accepted responsibility for Basque teaching programmes at all levels of education. In March 1980, the first Basque Parliament was elected, with Euskera recognized as an official language along with Spanish in the Basque provinces.

The Cambridge Encyclopaedia of Language
David Crystal, Cambridge University Press 1987

4 DISFIGURED ROAD SIGNS

Language and prejudice

1 CHATTER CHATTER?

> **TEACHER** Remember you have to give your talks to the class next lesson. You girls will be good at that, won't you! But we don't want too much scandal, do we, girls?

The word 'chatter' is usually used of women rather than men. It suggests **a** that women talk too much, and **b** that what women talk about is not important.

" It is undoubtedly female - the mouth is open."   *Daily Star*

a *Do women talk more than men?*
Many people believe that women talk more than men, but research shows that men talk much more than women. Men have been shown to talk more than women in staff meetings, in television panel discussions, and in husband and wife pairs. In one experiment, people were asked to describe three pictures. On average the men took 13 minutes per picture, and the women took three minutes and 17 seconds.

b *Do women talk about unimportant things?*
Women and men do *discuss different topics. Men often talk about sport, politics and cars, while women often talk about personal relationships, and bringing up children.*

Adapted from *Women, Men and Language* by Jennifer Coates

She's a great little mover. So SMOOTH ~ hardly makes a sound. I'll let you take her out for a spin when we get back.

2 ARE 'GAME BOYS' FOR BOYS ONLY?

This analysis of Nintendo 'Game Boy' games was prepared by a year 7 pupil from the list of games advertised by one mail order company.

Title of game	Main character	Who is saved?	Other comment
Alleyway			Depicts male character on box
Balloon Kid	F	M	
Bart Simpson in Escape from Camp Deadly	M		With little sister
Batman	M		
Boulder Dash	M		
Boxxle	M		Depicted as a male on box
Bubble Ghost	?		
Bugs Bunny (The Crazy Castle)	M	F	Bugs has to rescue Honey Bunny
Burai Fighter Deluxe	M		
Castlevania Adventure	M	F	
Double Dragon	M	F	
Dr Mario	M		
Duck Tales	M		
Dyna Blaster	M		
F-1 Race	M		If you win, women come and hug you
Fortified Zone	M F		
Gargoyles Quest	M		
Ghostbusters 2	4M		
Golf			Player depicted as male on box
Gremlins 2	M		
Hyperlode Runner	?		
Kick Off	22M		
Kung Fu Master	M		
Kwirk	M		You are a (male) tomato
Motocross Maniacs			You can't see what sex you are
Navy Seals	M		
Nemesis			You play a spaceship
Nintendo World Cup	22M		
Othello			Counter game
Rescue of Princess Blobette	M	F	
Qix			Strategy
R-Type			You play a spaceship
Radar Mission	M		You play a submarine
Revenge of the Gator			Pinball
Robocop	M	F	In level 2 you save a female hostage
Samurai Adventure	M		
Side Pocket			Snooker
Skate or Die (Bad 'n Rad)	M	F	
Solar Striker			You play a spaceship
The Amazing Spiderman	M		
Super Marioland	M	F	
Super RC pro am			You drive a radio controlled car
Teenage Mutant Hero Turtles (Fall of the Foot Clan)	4M	F	
Tennis			Depicted as male on the box
Wizards & Warriors (Fortress of Fear)	M	F	
WWF Superstars	M		

The same pupil counted all the pictures of people in the March edition of *TOTAL!* magazine, which is entirely devoted to Nintendo games:
Number of identifiable figures in pictures: Male [398] Female [39]

The only words spoken by a female figure were: 'At last, Baggie, our very own page! (Does my hair look all right?)'.

Game for a lass

Amongst the TOTAL! spy network, rumour has it (and it *is* only rumour you understand) that a new version of the massively successful cute-yet-def Game Boy is to be launched.

Called the Game Girl, the machine will have only one major difference from the version that is already conquering the pockets of game freaks across the planet – it will be pink.

Aside from this change – which is meant to appeal to girlies because everyone knows girls like pink (oh yeah?) – the games played will be exactly the same. It's hoped that this change of style won't mean that we'll soon be seeing softy titles like Terminator 3: Pillow Fight, My Little Pony Wars, Low Hem-Line Man and Skate Or Stay In.

TOTAL! Issue 2, February 1992

3 EXCLUSIVE LANGUAGE

Sometimes the words people use seem to exclude women:

> # Go to your
> # FIAT DEALER
> # today.
> # Tell him
> # NORMAN
> # sent you.

Newspaper advertisement

In *Walkabout*, two white children are contrasted with an aboriginal boy:

> It was very different with the aboriginal. He knew what reality was. He led a way of life that was already old when Tutankhamun started to build his tomb; a way of life that had been tried and proved before the white man's continents were even lifted out of the sea. Among the secret water-holes of the Australian desert his people had lived and died, unchanged and unchanging for twenty thousand years. Their lives were unbelievably simple. They had no homes, no food, no possessions. The few things they had, they shared: food and wives; children and laughter; tears and hunger and thirst.

From Walkabout *by James Vance Marshall*

> *This report book must be signed by your Year Master each day.*

Report book, comprehensive school

(In this school, three out of five 'Year Masters' were women.)

Dear Sir

This is commonly used as a greeting on letters where the name (and gender) of the person receiving the letter is unknown.

Pupils in a year 7 geography class all wrote letters to local industries asking for information. Out of 20 pupils, five opened their letters with 'Dear Sir', 15 opened their letters with 'Dear Sir or Madam', and none opened their letters with 'Dear Madam'. The majority of their replies were from women.

Comprehensive school

EQUALITY STYLE GUIDE

Most newspapers, magazines and books discriminate against women so automatically it is almost unconscious.
Here are suggestions for avoiding bias:

Instead of	Try
businessman	business manager, executive, boss, business chief, head of firm etc, businesswoman/people
cameraman	photographer, camera operator
newsman	journalist or reporter
fireman/men	firefighter, fire service staff, fire crews
dustman	refuse collector
foreman	supervisor
ice cream man	ice cream seller
policeman/men	police officer, or (pl) just police
salesman/girl	assistant, shop worker, shop staff, sales staff
steward/ess air hostess	airline staff, flight attendant
chairman	chairperson/woman, in the chair was . . . who chairs the committee
best man for the job	best person/woman . . .
man or mankind	humanity, human race, humans, people
manhood	adulthood
man-in-the-street	average citizen, average worker
manpower	workers, workforce, staffing
manning	staffing, jobs, job levels
manmade	synthetic, artificial, manufactured
Ford men voted . . .	Ford workers voted
male nurse	nurse
woman doctor	doctor
housewife	often means shopper, consumer, the cook
mothers	often means parents
girls (of over 18)	women (especially in sport)
spinster/divorcee	these words should not be used as an insult
he, his	sentence constructions can be changed to use they or theirs
Mrs, Miss	offer women the choice of being called Ms
John Smith and his wife Elsie	Elsie and John Smith
authoress	author – avoid /ess where possible
dolls, birds, ladies, Mrs Mopp pin ups	these, and puns arising from them are not funny are they really news?
spokesman	official, representative

Clause 10, Code of Conduct: A journalist shall neither originate nor process material which encourages discrimination on grounds of race, colour, creed, gender or sexual orientation.

Try the double standard test – would you use this description of a man?

Published by NUJ Equality Council, Acorn House, 314/320 Grays Inn Road, London WCI.

Sticks and stones – language which hurts

*'Sticks and stones can break my bones
But words can never hurt me.' (Proverb)*

1 WHAT KIND OF NAMES DO PEOPLE CALL EACH OTHER?

When people want to hurt me, they tease me about my religion, mainly because I do and believe things which are different to them. At first it made me upset and angry, now I just ignore them and keep out of their way.

They say things like 'you smell' or 'you're a user'

People call names to do with the way you look or talk, or your religion

twerp, wartbreath, moron, buttface, cow egghead, pig features, slob, trash face, rubber lugs, big lips, goofy, smoker, spacca.

lappo, duckhead, scruff, spacca.

Swot, slag, bitch, tight, cow, puff, spotty, four-eyes, grass, cry-baby, teacher's pet, shorty, scruff

If you're small they call you shorty or shrimp. People call me lanky, but I'm not bothered.

Egghead, softy, beala, lugsy, curtains.

Stupid, fat, ugly, retarded

hippie, scruff, thick.

They skit you about your appearence. They call you slut, slag, hussy, whore, dirty, scaly. They normally put 'fat' in front of it.

People say skits like Popeye, upperlip, mountain, cheeseneck, Huxley Pig.

People call me 'fat slut' even though I am neither, and because I wear glasses for class work I sometimes get called 'gigsy'.

The name-calling tends to be about a physical disfigurement / where they live / how they speak / if their parents are separated or divorced. They will say "At least I have a dad", and so on.

2 WHICH NAMES HURT MOST?

Fat, ugly, big mouth hurts most.

When people say things about your family.

Things like crawler or user.

The ones your best friend calls you behind your back.

my nicknames: Lips, Lipsy, Big Lips

When I was small I had to have hearing aids and people kept making fun of me

Swear words hurt most.

The names people say are things about my family and me. "Spacka" hurts most because my brother has cerebral palsy. They make songs up about me. One day I was at music and I heard people talk about my brother. I had to walk out of the classroom. It hurts very deep down inside of me. I have lots of name-calling, and if I tell my mam we can talk for hours and we get it sorted out.

The name that hurts me most is 'upper lip'. It makes me feel like running away

It hurts loob when you get called stupid

Names that hurt most are ones about your appearance.

They skit you about things like your dad not living with your mum. The names that hurt are about dad, - it feels as if your lonely.

When people call hurtful names at others, it's usually things that are at least part true. These are names that hurt most because you tend to believe them.

if it's someone you care about, you feel betrayed
If it's someone else, it doesn't hurt as much

When I came to this school I was skitted by them and they said one I have never told anyone before. They said 'Hey spacka, is your wrist hurting from slapping it?'

Names about something which is not true are worst.

It makes you sad and you feel lonely.

It feels very hurtful and lonely.

You get this feeling inside like your heart's half up your throat, and you want to start crying.

It feels awful.

It feels horrible, and you feel like hitting them sometimes.

I get a burning feeling inside and I get all hot and flustered

It feels horrible and upsetting, like a constant headache.

People call me names like 'elf' just because I'm small. It's mainly boys who call me names. It hurts, not like being hit, but like you have just lost a friend. I feel like crying, but I try not to.

It feels awful. I start to cry, or not to cry because if you cry they say it to you all the time.

You feel as if you're in the wrong, you've done something to insult people, such as be fat or spotty, when really it's them in the wrong, because you can't help being fat or whatever. You feel as if you kill yourself when people call you names. Sometimes I cry not to go to school because of the kids.

It feels horrible, you feel like crying & running out of room, your face starts to burn and you get this feeling right at the bottom of your stomach.

I just try to ignore it and pretend that it doesn't hurt, but it does really.

If I've been called names I've either kept quiet until they've shut up, or lost my temper and answered them back ... neither usually works.

> *All these statements were made by pupils in years 7, 8, and 9 at a comprehensive school.*

H The language of prayer

Arti

Arti is a special prayer. It is usually sung while the arti lamp is moved in a circular movement in front of the deity, as a sign of purity and a symbol of prayer going up to God.

O Lord of the Universe, Supreme Soul, Dispeller of sorrow, hail to Thee! May Thy rule of righteousness be established everywhere for it is Thou who banisheth in an instant the agonies of Thy devotees. May Thy kingdom of virtue reign supreme.

Whoever meditates upon Thee receives Thy grace. The worries of his mind disappear; his home is blessed with peace, happiness and plenty and all his bodily pains vanish.

Thou art my Mother and Father. Who else's protection can I seek? Besides Thee there is no other in whom I can place my hope.

Thou art God perfect, the knower of our innermost thought, the Most Exalted Master of all.

Thou art an Ocean of Mercy, the Protector of all. I am Thy servant, Thou my master. Grant me Thy grace.

Thou art beyond the knowledge of the senses, Formless the Lord of all life! Grant me wisdom that I may have a glimpse of Thee!

Thou art the Friend of the helpless and the Dispeller of suffering. Thou art my Saviour. Extend Thy hand of mercy. I seek Thy refuge.

Destroy our base desires and wipe out our sins, increase our faith and devotion. May we serve Thee and Thy devotees!

आरती

ॐ जय जगदीश हरे स्वामी जय जगदीश हरे ।
भक्तजनों के संकट क्षण में दूर करे ॥ ॐ

जो ध्यावे फल पावे दुःख विनशे मन का ॥
सुख सम्पत्ति घर आवे कष्ट मिटे तन का ॥ ॐ

मात-पिता तुम मेरे शरण गहूँ किसकी ।
तुम बिन और न दूजा आस करूं जिसकी ॥ ॐ

तुम प्ररण परमात्मा तुम अन्तर्यामी ।
पारब्रह्मा परमेश्वर तुम सबके स्वामी ॥ ॐ

तुम करुणा के सागर तुम पालन कर्ता ।
मैं मूरख खल कामी कृपा करो भर्ता ॥ ॐ

तुम हो एक अगोचर सबके प्राणपति ।
किस विधि मिलूं दयामय तुमको मैं कुमति ॥ ॐ

दीनबन्धु दुःख हर्ता तुम ठाकुर मेरे ।
करुणा हस्त बढ़ाओ द्वार पड़ा तेरे ॥ ॐ

विषय विकार मिटाओ पाप हरो देवा ।
श्रध्दा भक्ति बढ़ाओ सन्तन की सेवा ॥ ॐ

Official language

1 OVERDUE BILL

British
TELECOM

Reminder for Payment

Customer account number

NEWCASTLE
NORTH EAST

NE 1685 0777 Q010
30/03/1992 GO

---- SWAN HOUSE
157 PILGRIM STREET
NEWCASTLE UPON TYNE
NE1 1BA

IF YOU HAVE A QUERY ABOUT
THIS BILL

OUR CUSTOMER RECEPTIONISTS
WILL BE PLEASED TO HELP YOU
CALL FREE OF CHARGE ON
150

MONDAY-SATURDAY 8.00-6.00PM

TELEPHONE NUMBER: TYNESIDE

May we draw your attention to the invoice that we recently
sent to you, and which our records show to be overdue.

If your payment is already on its way to us and has
overlapped with this reminder, please accept our apologies
for having troubled you.

If you have not already paid, may we please have immediate
payment by post, to the address on the counterfoil, or in
---- person at your local Phoneshop. If not, regrettably, we
may have to consider disconnecting your service at the
Exchange. Please read the notes on disconnection overleaf.

Please note that if your service is disconnected, the
reconnection fee is £32.80 plus £8.98 per extra line
(both amounts exclusive of VAT).

Please pay this amount   £   60.23

Western Water Ltd

Smithson Industrial Estate
Bath, Avon
BA3 2JD
Telephone: (0200) 100300

W E S T E R N
W A T E R L T D

Serving the West

TO THE OCCUPIER

NOTICE IS HEREBY GIVEN that owing to repair of mains the water supply to your premises will be off from 8.30 am for approximately 4 hours on 11 APR 1991 but no notice of the resumption of supply will be issued.

UNTIL THE WATER SUPPLY IS RESTORED KEEP ALL TAPS CLOSED and you are advised to **REMOVE PLUGS FROM SINKS, HAND BASINS, BATHS etc. DO NOT DRAW OFF WATER THROUGH HOT TAPS.**

After the interruption times stated above, (or if you are in doubt that the water is back on again) please **TURN ON AT THE COLD TAP** before making enquiries.

What to look for

You may find some of the following ideas helpful when you are discussing the cuttings:

Power relationships

The way we speak or write changes according to who it is we are speaking or writing to, and why it is we are speaking or writing. It is very interesting to see how language changes according to the status or power of the person we are speaking to.

Power relationships may be due to:

age
you (−) speaking to your parents (+)
you (+) speaking to a baby (−)

status
you (−) speaking to a teacher (+)
headteacher (+) speaking to a teacher (−)

knowledge
you (−) speaking to your geography teacher (+)
about geography
you (+) speaking to your geography teacher (−) about
your hobby

physical power
you (−) speaking to the class bully (+)
what do you (−) call a gorilla with a machine gun (+)?

Key: (+) = more powerful   (−) = less powerful

Power relationships are not always the same. You will speak to your parents differently if you are complaining (asserting *your* status), or if you are asking for help (recognising *their* status).

Making rules

Power relationships are not only shown in the way in which we speak to other people. They are also shown in the rules about who is allowed to speak, and how, and when. The rules will usually favour the more powerful person, and they may even be controlled by the more powerful person.

Think about school. Your teachers control:

- when you are allowed to speak in class
- who you are allowed to speak to in class
- what you are allowed to speak about in class
- how loudly you are allowed to speak in class.

There are also rules about what teachers can say in lessons, and how:

- they wouldn't usually tell lies
- they wouldn't usually swear
- they can't talk for too long about things which are not relevant to the lesson
- they can't say nothing for the whole lesson.

Power and prejudice

Although it is quite normal for there to be power differences between speakers, there are some situations where the power differences arise from prejudice. Prejudice may be based on:

social class
people sometimes assume that if you speak with a 'posh' accent you are more intelligent than if you speak with a local accent

ethnic groups
many people show their prejudices through the way they speak to and about people of other ethnic groups

gender
men interrupt women much more often than women interrupt men

fitness
people with disabilities often complain that able-bodied people ignore them or speak to them indirectly: 'Does s/he take sugar?'.

Some prejudices are so strong and have been around for so long that they have become built into the language. For example:

- Some people use the pronoun 'he' to mean 'he or she'. They never use 'she' in the same way.
- People often assume that someone doing an important job is a man. For example, they might expect a doctor to be a man, and if the doctor were a woman they would say 'woman doctor'.

General activities

1 Power relationships (1)

Look at the examples of power relationships given on page 21. Talk about each example with a friend, and relate it to your own experience, for example: how do you speak to your parents? how do they speak to you? You may find it helpful to act out some of the conversations. Find more examples under each of the four headings of age, status, knowledge and physical power.

2 Power relationships (2)

Working with a friend, think about all the people you have talked to in the past two days. Draw three columns on a sheet of paper and make a list of the times when you have been more powerful, the times when you have been equal, and the times when you have been less powerful. In each case, explain the power relationship in terms of age, status or knowledge. What do you think happens when power relationships overlap, for example when someone of high status talks to someone who is of lower status, but older and more knowledge-able? Can you give examples of this from your own experience?

3 Power relationships (3)

Collect as many examples as you can of writing which is addressed to you. It might be letters, notes, textbooks, newspapers, advertise-ments, teachers' comments on your work, notices in school, and so on. Sort them into three groups: those where you are powerful, those where you are addressed as an equal, and those where the writer is powerful. In each case can you explain the power relationship in terms of age, status or knowledge?

4 Rules at home

What are the rules about speaking in your household? Who makes them? Are the rules the same for all the family? Think about some of the following questions:

- when and where can you shout?
- are there times or places where you have to whisper?
- are there times or places where you may not whisper?
- who makes the rules for your bedroom?
- who makes the rules for the lounge?

- are there special rules for meal-times?
- do the rules change if there are visitors?
- do the rules change at night?
- who is allowed to swear? when? how much?
- are there any things you are not allowed to talk about?
- are there any things you *must* say? (for example, 'please', 'thank you')
- who is allowed to use local dialect? when?
- can you use slang?

You might present your list as 'Rules for parents' and 'Rules for children', or you might draw a plan of the house and show the rules for each room – be adventurous!

5 Rules in society

Work with a friend to discuss who makes the rules about who can speak and how and when in each of the following situations:

- in a religious service
- in the playground
- in a courtroom
- at an auction
- in a school assembly
- at meal-times
- in a sports match
- at the dentist's.

What are the rules in each case? What happens when the rules are broken?

6 Breaking the rules

Work with a group to act out what happens when someone breaks the rules about speaking. It might be a young child, a new pupil, your loud and talkative friend, or someone wanting to make trouble.

You could choose to concentrate on one rule, or to have them break as many rules as possible.

Language at school

1 Teacher/pupil conversations

People studying language have suggested that the way teachers talk to pupils is very strange! For example:

- teachers often ask questions when they already know the answers
- teachers often ask questions for which there is only one 'right' answer
- teachers often repeat the answers that are given to their questions
- teachers often encourage the pupil by saying 'yes' or 'well done' if the answer is right
- teachers often add details to the answers they are given.

EXPLORATION

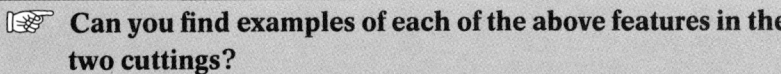

☞ **Can you find examples of each of the above features in the two cuttings?**

☞ **Try reading the two conversations aloud with one of you as the teacher and one of you as the pupil. Now read them again, but with the 'teacher' reading the 'pupil's' lines and the 'pupil' reading the 'teacher's' lines. What do you think would happen if you spoke to one of your teachers like that?**

☞ **How fair is the description of the way in which teachers talk? Do any of your own teachers do this? Why do you think teachers might choose to talk in this way?**

ACTIVITY 1

Work with a group to explore scenes where a teacher talks like this all the time: to pupils, to parents, to the headteacher, to the doctor, to shop assistants, to the cat, to him/herself . . .

ACTIVITY 2

Work with a group to explore what might happen if a pupil talked like this to the teacher . . .

2 Lost for words

This is a real example of a conversation between a pupil and a teacher.

EXPLORATION

 Act out the conversation. Explore the ways in which the teacher uses his voice and gestures.

 How does the teacher exert power in the conversation? Which rules for speaking is the boy being made to follow?

ACTIVITY 1

Find out about the rules for talking to teachers in your own school:

• are they different for different teachers?

• are they different for different pupils (such as year 7 and year 11 girls and boys)?

• what are the rules for teachers talking to the headteacher?

ACTIVITY 2

Act out or rewrite the conversation, making the teacher helpful and encouraging to the pupil.

ACTIVITY 3

Rewrite the conversation as if it were part of a novel, showing each character's thoughts and feelings at each stage.

3 Handbook for new pupils

This cutting is taken from a handbook issued to all new year 7 pupils at a comprehensive school.

EXPLORATION

 Talk about the list with a friend. Look at:

• Which words you would expect to hear from teachers, but not so much from other pupils?

• Why have some words been written in BLOCK CAPITALS?

• Which of the rules control the language which the pupils must use?

- Do the same rules apply in your school?
- Are the rules sensible and reasonable?
- Do you think that adults would allow someone to control their language in this way?

ACTIVITY 1

Try rewriting the rules in a much 'friendlier' way. For example, you could explain each rule, or introduce the word 'please'.

ACTIVITY 2

Rewrite the rules in a much sterner tone. For example, try outlining the punishments for anyone who disobeys.

Commands and requests

1   No smoking signs

EXPLORATION

☞ **What is the tone of each of the signs: polite? helpful? stern? threatening? List them in order from the most friendly to the least friendly. Explain what it is about each sign that makes it friendly or unfriendly.**

☞ **Where do you think each of these signs has been found?**

☞ **List the signs in order from the most effective to the least effective. What makes a 'no smoking' sign effective?**

☞ **Compare your list of friendly/unfriendly signs with your list of effective/ineffective signs. Do they match in any way?**

ACTIVITY 1

Make your own collection of no smoking signs and other signs that give you commands or requests (for example, no trespassing signs, no parking signs, litter signs, and so on).

For each sign note down:

- where it is sited
- what you think the tone of the sign is
- how large it is
- how effective you think the sign is.

ACTIVITY 2

Work with a group to design your own no smoking signs:

- for use in a private home
- for use in a school staffroom
- for use in pupils' toilets
- for use in a restaurant
- for use in a place of your own choice.

In each case explain why you think your sign would be effective in that setting.

Language that lets you do things

1 Banknote

EXPLORATION

 **Look closely at the banknote shown.**

- How many different typefaces are shown on it?

- Why do you think these different typefaces are used?

- Think about each piece of writing on the note: who is the writer? who is the audience? How many different writers and audiences can you find?

- What are all the pictures and patterns for?

ACTIVITY 1

Try to obtain some banknotes in other currencies. (Friends or their parents may have them left over from holidays abroad.) Compare them as closely as you can with the British banknote shown.

ACTIVITY 2

Try to obtain some toy money, for example from a board game. Compare it with the real money you have looked at.

ACTIVITY 3

Design your own banknote.

2 *Rail tickets*

EXPLORATION

 Look closely at the tickets shown.

- Why do you think the ticket is overprinted with the words 'British Rail' so often and in such tiny letters?

- Look at each word written on the front of the ticket: what does it mean? who is supposed to read it? what do you think the numbers mean? who is supposed to read them?

- Look at the words on the back of the ticket. Are there any words that are unusual or unfamiliar to you? what do they mean? who is supposed to read this information? what is the black line for? what do you think all the numbers mean? who might they be written for?

ACTIVITY 1

Collect as many other tickets as you can: bus tickets, cinema tickets, Metro or Underground tickets, raffle tickets, dinner tickets, any tickets. Compare the tickets you collect with the rail tickets shown here. How do you know they are tickets? Are there any features which all the tickets have in common? What differences are there between the tickets?

ACTIVITY 2

Prepare a display called 'The language of tickets'. Use arrows and labels to show the similarities and differences between the tickets in your display.

ACTIVITY 3

What do you think makes a good ticket? Draw up a list of five qualities a good ticket should have. Give each of the tickets you have collected a score out of 10 for each of the five qualities you have chosen. Which do you consider is the best ticket? Write to the organisation that produced the best ticket, and congratulate them, explaining why you thought their ticket was so good, or write to the organisation that produced the worst ticket to tell them what was wrong with it.

'Bad' language?

1 Punch *cartoon*

EXPLORATION

☞ **What is there in what the old lady says that suggests she is not talking to an equal?**

☞ **This cartoon was published 80 years ago. Do you think we have the same attitude to children swearing today? Would a modern child just go ahead and swear? Why do you think there are different rules for adults and for children?**

2 *Four letters and the law*

EXPLORATION

☞ **Do you think Eric Partridge was right to include 'fuck' in his dictionary? Why do you think people find 'f***' less offensive than writing the full word? Which form do you think is right? Do you think people were right to complain to schools and public libraries?**

ACTIVITY 1

Imagine you are the librarian in a large public library. A local councillor has written to you complaining about Partridge's dictionary, and asking you to remove it from your shelves. Write a reply explaining whether you have removed it and why you made your decision.

ACTIVITY 2

Ask the librarian in your local library whether or not they have Partridge's dictionary. Ask them to explain their policy on books containing swear words. Would they stock a book with a swear word on the cover? Ask the same questions in your library at school.

3 *Tax tuft cost £60*

EXPLORATION

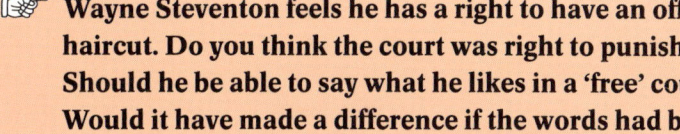 **Wayne Steventon feels he has a right to have an offensive haircut. Do you think the court was right to punish him? Should he be able to say what he likes in a 'free' country? Would it have made a difference if the words had been on his T-shirt or on a banner? Would it have made a difference if the words were only visible at 10 metres?**

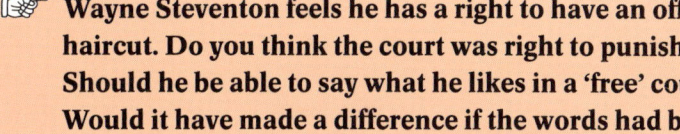 **The newspaper article used the same words that Wayne Steventon used. Why do you think it is all right for the newspaper to use the words, but not Mr Steventon?**

ACTIVITY 1

Act out the scene in court.

ACTIVITY 2

Act out or describe what would happen in your own school if a pupil had an offensive haircut.

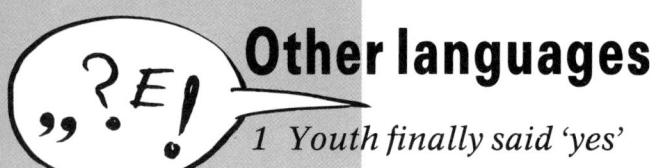 **Other languages**

1 Youth finally said 'yes'

The word 'aye' is commonly used instead of 'yes' in Scotland and in north-east England. (Whitley Bay is in north-east England.) It is a very old word, which was used by Shakespeare in his plays, in the Authorised Version of the Bible, and which is still used today in Parliament.

EXPLORATION

> **Work with a group to act out the court scene. Then talk together about the following:**
>
> - Why do you think that the youth was being so awkward?
>
> - Why do you think that the magistrates objected to the word 'aye'?
>
> - Do you think that the court was right to make so much fuss over one word?
>
> **Do people ever object to the language you use, your dialect or your slang? Which words do they object to? How does it feel to have your language 'corrected'? Do you ever behave like the youth in court?**

ACTIVITY 1

Act out the discussion between the youth and his solicitor at the police station. How does she persuade him to apologise?

ACTIVITY 2

Act out conversations between the youth and his parents, and the youth and his schoolfriends. How does he explain his behaviour?

ACTIVITY 3

Make lists of:

- people who object to your language or dialect
- situations where people criticise your language or dialect
- words that people object to.

Explain when you think it's all right to criticise someone's language, and when you think it's wrong to do so.

2 Mind how you say it

EXPLORATION

 Talk about the incident described. Do you believe it really happened like that? Are there any words that you would use to test outsiders in the same way?

ACTIVITY 1

Act out the scene at the river. Try to imagine how each of your characters feel about what they are doing.

ACTIVITY 2

Imagine that you are an Ephraimite fugitive. Tell the story of how you managed to cross the river.

ACTIVITY 3

Write a story in which someone is given away by their accent or pronunciation.

3 Basque

EXPLORATION

 Why do you think the Spanish government wanted to ban the use of the Basque language? How do you think the Basque people felt about it?

ACTIVITY 1

Use your school library to find out about the Basque Separatist Movement (ETA).

ACTIVITY 2

Work with a group to develop one of the following situations into a short play:

- a public burning of Basque books
- someone being arrested for speaking Basque in public

- two parents being prevented from using a Basque name at the baptism of their child

- grandparents' Basque names being removed from their tombstones.

4 Disfigured road sign

EXPLORATION

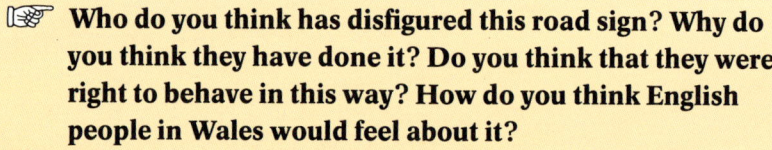 **Who do you think has disfigured this road sign? Why do you think they have done it? Do you think that they were right to behave in this way? How do you think English people in Wales would feel about it?**

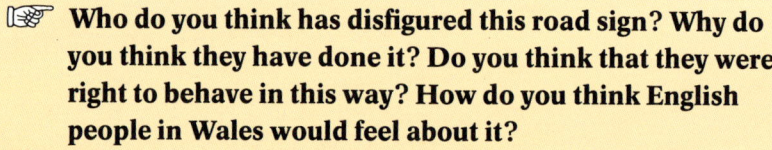 **Have you come across road signs treated like this in Wales or anywhere else?**

ACTIVITY 1

Imagine you have been caught changing a road sign from English to Welsh. How would you explain what you have done to the police? Act out or describe what happens.

ACTIVITY 2

Imagine you are a magistrate trying someone who has disfigured a road sign. What will you say to them if they are convicted? What punishment will you impose?

 Language and prejudice

1 Chatter chatter?

EXPLORATION

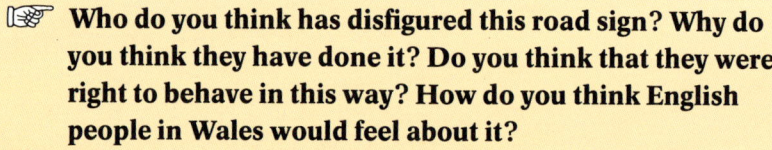 **Compare the teacher's comment and the *Daily Star* cartoon with the views given by Jennifer Coates. What do you think?**

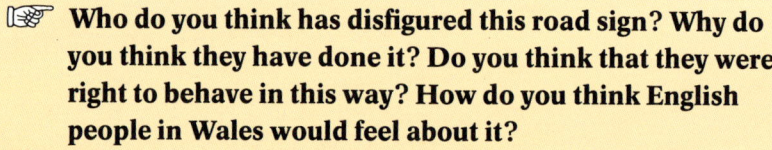 **Many people believe that women talk more than men, but research shows the exact opposite. How can you explain this?**

ACTIVITY 1

Conduct your own research into men and women talking. You could observe boys and girls in your class, or your parents, or people on television. You will need to decide what sort of information you want and how you are going to measure it.

ACTIVITY 2

Collect as many examples as you can of people assuming either that women talk too much, or that what women talk about is unimportant. Display the evidence with your comments on it. Do you think it is possible to change people's attitudes?

2 Are 'Game Boys' for boys only?

EXPLORATION

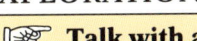 Talk with a friend about the evidence shown. Why do you think there are so few games with women as the main characters? Why do you think it is usually women who are rescued? Do you think it matters that women are either left out of games or only shown in one way? Do a survey to find out how the boys in your class would feel if the machines were called 'Game Girls', all the main characters were women, and men were only there to be rescued.

 Do you think that pink 'Game Girls' will appeal to 'girlies'? What do you think of the girls' games suggested?

ACTIVITY 1

Make your own analysis of 'Game Boy' games or of games for other similar machines. Do your results agree with the ones shown here?

ACTIVITY 2

Make your own analysis of a games magazine. Do your results confirm the ones shown here?

ACTIVITY 3

Write to a games company or a games magazine and give your opinion on how girls or women are shown.

3 Exclusive language

EXPLORATION

> **Read each of the quotations aloud, and discuss them. Do you think it matters that 'man' is used to mean 'men and women' or that 'he' is used to mean 'he or she'?**

ACTIVITY 1

Collect your own examples of statements which exclude women.

ACTIVITY 2

Rewrite each of the statements to make them more acceptable.

ACTIVITY 3

Compare the quotations with the NUJ Equality Style Guide on page 13. Which guidelines are broken?

4 Equality Style Guide

EXPLORATION

> **How helpful do you find the advice given in the NUJ's Equality Style Guide? Are there any suggestions that you disagree with? Do you have any suggestions to add? Do you think that journalists actually follow this advice? Find evidence in local and national newspapers.**

ACTIVITY 1

Listen to the news on the radio or on television. How often is a word like 'businessmen' used when 'business people' would be more acceptable?

ACTIVITY 2

Look at a newspaper. Can you find any examples of where the Equality Style Guide would help the journalist to write more fairly? Rewrite any sentences that need to be improved. Are some newspapers better than others at avoiding prejudice?

Sticks and stones – language that hurts

Name-calling is a very sensitive issue. Don't attempt to work on this section unless you are sure that you can talk seriously about it, and respect the feelings of other people.

EXPLORATION

☞ **What do you think of the proverb 'sticks and stones'? *Can* words hurt?**

☞ **Talk about the names given in the book. Are the same names used at your own school?**

☞ **Talk about the statements dealing with which words hurt most. Which ones do you agree with? Are there any suggestions you would add?**

☞ **Talk about the descriptions of how it feels to be called names. Which describes it best for you?**

☞ **Talk about why people call each other names.**

☞ **What can you do if people are calling you names? What should parents and teachers do if children are being bullied in this way?**

ACTIVITY 1

Imagine that one or more of these children has come to you for advice. Write, act, or record the advice you would give.

ACTIVITY 2

The statements were taken from a survey of 50 pupils at the same comprehensive school. What advice would you give to teachers and pupils at this school? Act out a meeting of house heads or year heads where the statements are discussed.

ACTIVITY 3

Write a story or a poem which explores what it is like for a child who is being called names.

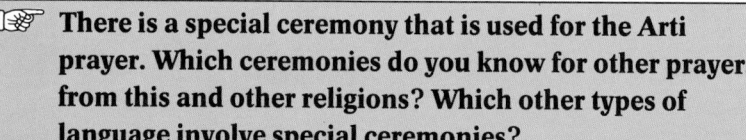

The language of prayer

Prayer is the language people use when they are talking to the most powerful being they know – their god.

EXPLORATION

> ☞ **There is a special ceremony that is used for the Arti prayer. Which ceremonies do you know for other prayers from this and other religions? Which other types of language involve special ceremonies?**
>
> ☞ **Talk about the language used. Look at:**
>
> - the names given to God
>
> - the use of capitals (in the English translation)
>
> - the use of old-fashioned words like 'thee' and 'thou' and 'banisheth' (in the English translation)
>
> - the fact that the prayer is sung.
>
> **How is the language of the prayer different from the language of a letter?**
>
> **What do you think is the tone of the prayer?**
>
> **How would you describe the purposes of the prayer?**

ACTIVITY 1

Collect examples of other prayers. Compare them with this prayer, and make a list of the similarities and differences. What can you find that is special about the language of prayer? How many different purposes can you find for prayers?

ACTIVITY 2

Work with a group to prepare questions about the language of prayer. Think about:

- the purposes of prayer
- ceremonies
- special words that are used for prayer
- the range of different prayers.

Use your questions to interview your RE teacher or local religious leaders.

Official language

1 Overdue bill

EXPLORATION

☞ **Talk about the style and tone of the letter. Look at:**

- The note welcoming queries (with a free phone line).

- Polite phrases like 'may we' and 'please accept our apologies' and 'may we please' and 'please note'.

- Why does it say 'If not, regrettably, we may have to consider disconnecting your service at the Exchange', rather than 'If you do not pay we will disconnect your telephone'?

- Which words or phrases seem particularly 'official'?

- Why is the letterhead printed in red?

☞ **Imagine first that you are someone who has already paid this bill, and then that you are someone who cannot afford to pay this bill. How will you respond to the letter in each case?**

☞ **The purpose of this letter is to make a threat. Do you think that the threat is more effective or less effective for being made so politely?**

ACTIVITY 1

Rewrite the letter in a more obviously threatening way.

ACTIVITY 2

Work with a partner. One of you reads aloud the letter as it is written in your most pleasant and courteous voice. The other repeats each sentence, but this time saying what it *really* means in a more threatening voice.

ACTIVITY 3

Compare this letter with the water supply letter on page 20. Which do you think is better? Why?

EXPLORATION

☞ **Talk about the style and tone of the letter:**

- Why is it addressed to 'the occupier' rather than to 'Mrs Bloggs'?

- Which words or phrases seem particularly 'official'?

- Why do you think it says 'the water supply to your premises will be cut off' instead of 'we have decided to switch off the water supply to your house'?

- Why are parts of the letter in capitals?

- What would happen if it were inconvenient to have your water cut off at that time?

- Why does the letter not apologise for the inconvenience that will be caused?

ACTIVITY 1

Write a more friendly and personal letter giving the same information.

ACTIVITY 2

Collect other examples of official letters or notices, and compare them with this letter.

ACTIVITY 3

Compare this letter with the overdue bill, on page 19. Which do you think is better? Why?